If I Designed the Zoo

by Noelle Disher
illustrated by George Ulrich

 HOUGHTON MIFFLIN BOSTON

Copyright © by Houghton Mifflin Company. All rights reserved.

No part of this work may be reproduced or transmitted in any form or by any means, electronic or mechanical, including photocopying or recording, or by any information storage or retrieval system without the prior written permission of Houghton Mifflin Company unless such copying is expressly permitted by federal copyright law. Address inquiries to School Permissions, Houghton Mifflin Company, 222 Berkeley Street, Boston, MA 02116.

Printed in China

ISBN 10: 0-618-89928-6
ISBN 13: 978-0-618-89928-9

23456789 NOR 16 15 14 13 12 11 10 09 08

Carlota, Ellis, and Luke were busy working on a class project. Each group needed to use what they had learned about perimeter and area in class to draw the plans for something. Carlota, Ellis, and Luke had decided to plan a zoo. They all went to the zoo as often as they could.

The three friends had read about different animals and had chosen some for their plan. Carlota, Ellis, and Luke wanted to make sure their animals had enough space to live well. They needed to show the size of each animal's home in their plans.

The friends knew they needed to show the area and the perimeter of each animal's home. They had learned that area is the number of square units that cover a surface area. Perimeter is the distance around a figure.

Their teacher had taught them about finding the area and perimeter of a figure. To find the area of each animal home, the three friends would need to multiply the length by the width of the home. To find the perimeter, they would need to add the lengths of all the home's sides together. Now they were ready to dig in!

Luke wanted to work on the meerkat home first. Meerkats are small animals that need room to dig tunnels and run around. This is what he drew:

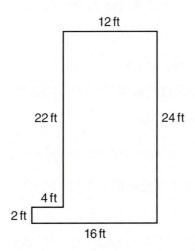

Read·Think·Write To find the perimeter of something, do you multiply or add the lengths?

The meerkat home was not a basic rectangle. To find the area, Luke divided the complex figure into two rectangles. Here is what he did:

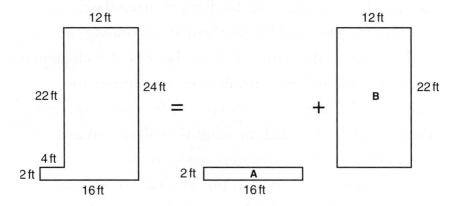

Luke was now ready to find the area, or square feet (ft²). For rectangle A, he multiplied the length by the width.

$$\text{Area} = l \times w$$
$$\text{rectangle A} = 2 \text{ ft} \times 16 \text{ ft}$$
$$\text{rectangle A} = 32 \text{ ft}^2$$

Luke figured the area for rectangle B.

$$\text{rectangle B} = 12 \text{ ft} \times 22 \text{ ft}$$

Read·Think·Write What is the area of rectangle B?

However, Luke was not finished yet. Now he needed to add the area for rectangle A and the area for rectangle B to find the total area of the figure.

Total area of the figure: 32 ft² + 264 ft² = 296 ft²

Ellis would find the perimeter for the meerkat home. He looked at the plan and thought about how he would figure it out. Ellis remembered that he needed to add all the sides of the figure together.

This is what he drew:

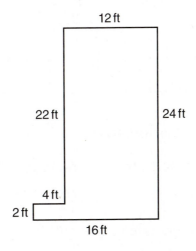

Perimeter = 12 ft + 24 ft + 16 ft + 2 ft + 4 ft + 22 ft = ?

Read·Think·Write What is the perimeter of the meerkat home?

Carlota wanted to draw the monkey home.

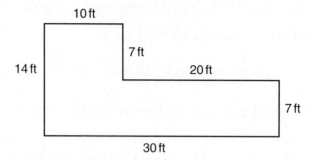

Next, Carlota worked on finding the area. She divided the figure into two rectangles.

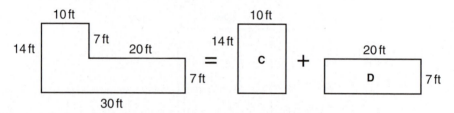

It was time for Carlota to do the math.

rectangle C = 10 ft × 14 ft
rectangle C = 140 ft²

rectangle D = 20 ft × 7 ft
rectangle D = 140 ft²

The area for rectangle C was 140 ft², and the area for rectangle D was 140 ft².

Read•Think•Write What is the total area for the monkey home?

Carlota and Luke worked together to find the perimeter of the monkey home.

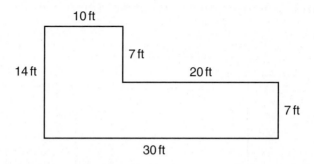

Perimeter = 10 ft + 7 ft + 20 ft + 7 ft + 30 ft + 14 ft = 88 ft

They were doing great! The perimeter of the monkey home would be 88 feet. The monkeys would have a lot of room to play and trees to climb on and swing from.

Luke was already working on another home. The next animal was the one that Luke liked best, so he knew just what to do.

Bears had always been Luke's favorite animal. Knowing that bears need a lot of room and a place to sleep in the winter, this is what he drew:

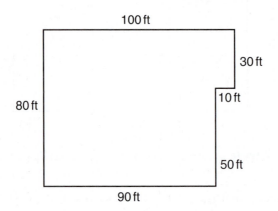

Next, Luke divided the complex figure into two rectangles to find the area of each.

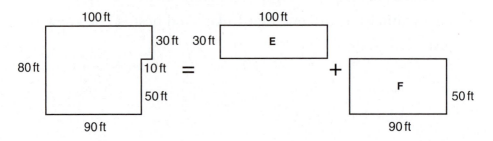

rectangle E = 100 ft × 30 ft   rectangle F = 90 ft × 50 ft

This bear home was going to be big!

Read·Think·Write What is the area of rectangle E? rectangle F? What is the total area of the bear home?

Ellis wrote an equation for the perimeter of the bear home.

Perimeter = 100 ft + 30 ft + 10 ft + 50 ft + 90 ft + 80 ft = 360 ft

Carlota, Ellis, and Luke agreed that this was a great plan for a zoo! All the animals would have the space they needed, and no two animal homes looked alike. This would make the zoo interesting for the people coming to see the animals, too.

Carlota and Luke talked more about the bear home, but Ellis was too excited about his favorite animal and the home he was going to draw next.

Ellis was lost in thought. He could just picture the elephants in their new home. He had read about the kinds of food elephants eat and about the large amount of space they need. When Ellis was done, he showed his plan to Carlota and Luke.

Ellis made a special design. This time, the complex figure needed to be divided into three rectangles to find the total area, or square yards (yd²):

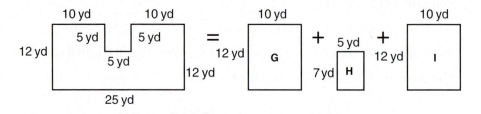

rectangle G = 10 yd × 12 yd   rectangle G = 120 yd²
rectangle H = 5 yd × 7 yd   rectangle H = 35 yd²
rectangle I = 10 yd × 12 yd   rectangle I = 120 yd²

Carlota added the three areas together to find the total area for the home.

Area of the complex figure = 120 yd² + 35 yd² + 120 yd² = ?

Read·Think·Write What is the total area of the elephant home?

Luke and Ellis added to find the perimeter of the elephant home.

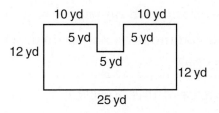

Perimeter = 10 yd + 5 yd + 5 yd + 5 yd + 10 yd
+ 12 yd + 25 yd + 12 yd = 84 yd

They had done it! The friends had used what they had learned in class to plan and draw zoo homes for their favorite animals.

They could see how important area and perimeter were when it came to making homes for animals. When Carlota, Ellis, and Luke went to the zoo next time, they compared their plans for animal homes to the zoo's animal homes. Then they spent the day dreaming of having their very own zoo!

Responding — Problem Solving

1. If you used rectangles B on page 4 and D on page 6 to make a new home for a zoo animal, what would the total area be?

2. What is the area of this object?

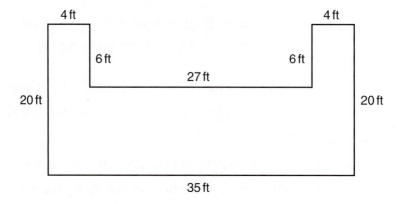

3. What is the perimeter of the object in question 2?

Activity

Visualize Work with a partner to plan a new shopping mall. All the stores in your plan must be complex figures, and you must have at least four stores. Find the area and perimeter for each store.